God Lives Next Door

Lyle K. Weiss

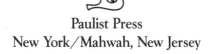

Paulist Press
New York/Mahwah, New Jersey

Cover/book design and interior illustrations by Nicholas T. Markell.

Library of Congress Cataloging-in-Publication Data

Weiss, Lyle K., 1966–
   God lives next door / Lyle K. Weiss.
      p.   cm.—(IlluminationBook)
   Includes bibliographical references.
   ISBN 0-8091-3842-5 (alk. paper)
   1. God—Biblical teaching. 2. Bible—Biography. I. Title. II. Series:
IlluminationBooks.
BS544.W44   1999
231—dc21   98-31706
                                                                      CIP

Published by Paulist Press
997 Macarthur Boulevard
Mahwah, New Jersey 07430

www.paulistpress.com

Printed and bound in the
United States of America

Contents

IlluminationBooks: A Foreword   vii

Preface   ix

Chapter One   1
  Experiencing God in the Ordinary
Chapter Two   16
  God Present in the Midst of Evil
Chapter Three   29
  God Works through Us All
Chapter Four   41
  God Recognized through Repentance
Chapter Five   50
  God Present in Love

Epilogue   61

Notes   64

Dedication

To my wife Terry, in thanksgiving for her love, through which I have recognized the presence and love of God.

Acknowledgments

Throughout the process of writing this book I was aware of my indebtedness to those who helped make this work a reality. In a special way I wish to thank Robert Wicks, the general editor of IlluminationBooks and a good friend, for his invitation to write this book and his belief that I had something worthwhile to say. I would like to thank Msgr. Joe Luca, dear friend and former pastor, who has encouraged and supported me and offered valuable suggestions concerning the book and life. I want to thank all of my scripture teachers over the years who have shared with me their love for God's Word. I hope that this text reveals something of the love I was fortunate to experience in them. Thanks also go to Maria Maggi, my editor at Paulist Press, for making the process such an easy, truly helpful, and enjoyable one. Fr. Chris Whatley, a new colleague, provided invaluable help as a reader with insightful suggestions, additions, and subtractions. Despite the contributions and insights of many, any shortcomings in the final text belong to me alone. This book is in some way a reflection of all those through whom God's love has been made known to me. It is my hope that the book does justice to the blessing their lives have been to me. Finally, I would like to thank my parents for their continued love and support through the years.

–Lyle K. Weiss
New Market, Maryland

IlluminationBooks

A Foreword

Whent this series was launched in 1994, I wrote that Illumination-Books were conceived to "bring to light wonderful ideas, helpful information, and sound spirituality in concise, illustrative, readable, and eminently practical works on topics of current concern."

In keeping with this premise, among the first books were offerings by well-known authors Joyce Rupp *(Little Pieces of Light...Darkness and Personal Growth)* and Basil Pennington *(Lessons from the Monastery That Touch Your Life)*. In addition, there were titles by up-and-coming authors and experts in the fields of spirituality and psychology. These books covered a wide array of topics: joy, controlling stress and anxiety, personal growth, discernment, caring for others, the mystery of the Trinity, celebrating the woman you are, and facing your own desert experiences.

The continued goal of the series is to provide great ideas, helpful steps, and needed inspiration in small volumes. Each of the books offers a new opportunity for the reader to explore possibilities and embrace practicalities that can be employed in everyday life. Thus, among the new and noteworthy themes for readers to discover are these: how to be more receptive to the love in our lives, simple ways to structure a personal day of recollection, a creative approach to enjoy reading sacred scriptures, and spiritual and psychological methods of facing discouragement.

Like the IlluminationBooks before them, forthcoming volumes are meant to be a source of support—without requiring an inordinate amount of time or prior preparation. To this end, each small work stands on its own. The hope is that the information provided not only will be nourishing in itself but also will encourage further exploration in the area.

When we view the world through spiritual eyes, we appreciate that sound knowledge is really useful only when it can set the stage for *metanoia*, the conversion of our hearts. Each of the IlluminationBooks is designed to contribute in some small but significant way to this process. So, it is with a sense of hope and warm wishes that I offer this particular title and the rest of the series to you.

–*Robert J. Wicks*
General Editor, IlluminationBooks

Preface

*I*f I point at the moon and you stare at my finger you will miss the moon entirely.[1]

How easy it would be to miss the moon because there are so many other things to look at. It is easy to get distracted by so many things in life that we can easily miss that for which we look.

Looking, or the desire to look, is not the only important aspect of a search. To find what you are looking for requires that you look in the right direction. No matter how hard you may be searching and how earnestly you desire to find the object of your search, you will be frustrated if you are not looking in the right direction. We need proper guidance if we are to find what it is for which we look.

Many in our world are engaged in the sincere search for God. And yet, for many, the search is fruitless. No matter how vigorously they look, the search for the presence of the divine in their lives and in the world appears to be in vain. As was just indicated, one possible reason for the fruitlessness of the search is not due to lack of desire, but to an inability to look in the right direction. To discover the presence of the Lord in our lives, we must allow our vision to be guided so that we may finally catch a glimpse of the moon rather than the pointing finger.

Many of the women and men in the Bible had profound experiences of God in their lives. The conscious awareness of this presence challenged and/or changed the way they viewed the world and the women and men with whom they shared it. But, God did not simply disappear when the last word of the Bible had been written. He continues to be present to us just as he was to the women and men whose names fill the pages of Scripture. We look back on their stories in hindsight, a hindsight that lessens our appreciation for the struggle they went through to know God in their lives. The Bible can serve as an indispensable guide in helping us appreciate their struggle, steering us in the right direction and focusing our attention in the direction of the God whom we seek.

Using the Bible as our guide requires a brief explanation concerning how Scripture can be fruitfully read. Modern biblical scholarship has greatly enhanced our ability to understand the time in which a biblical book was written, something of the identity of the community for whom it was written, and the theological vision the author wished to express. Beyond that, biblical scholarship provides insight into the faith experience that the biblical authors are attempting to capture by the way they relate the stories of God's saving activity. It is the intention of this book to approach the biblical texts at the level of the faith experience being conveyed.

The purpose of this book is to invite us to turn to the pages of Scripture to guide our attempts to recognize God's presence. Using the Bible as our guide, I would like to suggest five places we are encouraged to look in our quest for the Lord. In the first chapter, the figures of Moses and Elijah, as well as a sampling of recurring biblical symbols, will lead us to discover God in the ordinary of life. We all struggle with the existence and experience of evil and suffering in our lives and in the world. Thus, chapter 2 looks to Job and the apostle Paul as examples of faithfulness in spite of suffering. In the midst of their own experience of evil and suffering, they were able to perceive the presence of the God who was with them in their struggles. The third chapter calls upon the wisdom articulated in the stories of the great figures of the Hebrew Scriptures, the unknown descendants of Jesus and Mary, his mother. Their stories shine light on the God present in the fidelity of ordinary people responding to the Lord's call in their lives. Chapter 4 attempts to open our eyes and hearts to God's presence in the gift of repentance by reflecting on the connection the Bible makes between repentance and new life in God. Lastly, it is a central theme of Scripture that God is powerfully encountered in love. In the last chapter we will examine the life of John the Baptist and the structure of God's love revealed in the birth and death of Jesus to underline the Bible's insight regarding God's abiding presence in the willingness and action of love. St. Paul, in his First Letter to the Corinthians, reminds us that the Holy Spirit of God dwells within each of us (3:16). Only when we first recognize the presence of God in our own hearts can we open our lives to acknowledge his presence in the ways the Bible suggests.

At the end of each chapter I will include some Scripture passages as part of reflection exercises for the purpose of helping us to develop the habit of looking for God where the Bible reminds us he is most often found. It is my hope that the reflections in this book, as well as the exercises that conclude each chapter, will support our efforts as individuals and as communities, to discover God's presence in our lives and to allow his presence to shape us into instruments of his life and love.

Chapter One

Experiencing God in the Ordinary

We all want to know and feel the presence of God's love in our lives. And yet, for many believers the experience of absence seems to be more prevalent than the experience of presence. We struggle to find the peace that flows from knowing that God cares about what is going on, not only in the world, but in our personal lives as well. This search can be a frustrating attempt to discover something that seems to want to remain hidden. It is often like playing hide and seek with someone who can hide in places we can never reach. And so, while we conclude that God exists, we get the sense that he does not have a great deal to do with our lives and with our role in life. But this problem really does not so much reside with God as with the directions in which we look. The Bible can serve as an excellent guide for helping to recognize God's presence for those of us who strive to know him and the difference he can make in our lives. More specifically, the Bible can be an extraordinary guide in helping us to find him in those places we may not have otherwise looked. The Bible reveals to us a God who, more often than not, is recognized in the ordinary of life.

The search for God

God is active and present in our lives and world. And yet, for many believers, the life of faith seems to resemble grasping in the darkness more than living in God's light. We believe because we want and need to believe. We want God to exist and to love us even if we have had no personal experience of such love in our lives. In the absence of any personal experience we hold on to our wish. William James once said, "Our faith is faith in someone else's faith, and in the greatest matters this is most the case."[2] We believe very often because those we trust believe. But our belief is often maintained because we want it to be true; we want it to be real, even when such a reality seems to be the furthest thing from the truth. We want to believe, but our lack of personal experience keeps us at a safe distance. Rather than committing our lives to a God whom we have come to know personally, we choose to exist on the margins, hoping that what we have wished for comes true. Faith, for many, is more a wish than a commitment. It is a dream for what we *hope* is true rather than an openness to experience in a personal way what *is* true.

In our worst moments of doubt and uncertainty, we convince ourselves that our wish for God is merely self-deception, our doubt revealing to us that what we had wished for all along was a dream from which we are only now awakening. Looking around at our world and examining the many moments of our lives, we conclude that God does not really exist, or that he does exist but does not care about our lives and what happens to us. But, it seems that our nagging suspicions have more to do with us than with God. He is very active in our lives and world, but very often we can miss his presence because of our expectations. To experience his presence in our lives and world, we must first begin looking in the right places. In those moments of doubt and uncertainty, we can wonder why God was so much more obvious for the people who lived in biblical times. How could someone not believe when the sea parts in front of you, when prophets perform miracles, when friends rise from the dead? It would be easy to commit if God spoke to us in the same way he spoke with Moses or one of the prophets. The problem arises for us when we are not called to from bushes, when seas do not part, when the dead do not rise. In the absence of such miracles we question whether God still cares as he once did, if it is safe to trust, if it is worthwhile to commit our lives to seeking and doing God's will, whatever that will might be.

The wisdom of hindsight

In convincing ourselves that God can only be discovered in such miraculous ways, we too easily forget that we read the Bible with the wisdom that hindsight provides. Consider our own experiences in life. Take adolescence. The puzzle of adolescence seemed like an unfathomable mystery to many of us in the midst of the experience. And yet, removed from it by a number of years, we can look back on that time in our lives with a vision that allows us to penetrate the mystery and understand to a greater degree the pain and joy of our youth. In the same way the authors of the biblical books were able to convey in images the depth and power of their religious heritage. They were able to speak of their ancestors' experiences of God in ways that would help those who came after to understand and appreciate what they knew to be true: that God was active in history and in their history specifically. In hindsight, his presence seemed so obvious. But, for those who lived through it, the struggle to experience that presence was no less challenging than it is for us.

Destinations on the journey

Although it is true that we can seek love and friendship in the wrong places and in the wrong people, we can also seek God in all the wrong places unless we begin to seek him in the ordinary. If we look only in the extraordinary, we run the risk of being disappointed. But, more importantly, if we look only in the extraordinary, we lose the sense of God's abiding presence with us always. With such an expectation of the extraordinary, his presence is relegated to occasional acts of miraculous power that serve as reminders that he is still around. But these reminders hardly constitute expressions of an ongoing relationship of love between God and us. God, as Jesus promised, is with us always, but in order to experience and appreciate that presence we must be willing to seek him in the ordinary. Like any relationship, it may involve certain extraordinary moments on occasion, but most of the relationship is lived out day to day in the ordinary ways and routines of life. The fact that our relationship with God is lived out in much the same way makes a commitment to him very difficult for those who seek him only in the extraordinary and earth shattering.

It is not surprising that in our day and age, when the validity in being a Christian has come under such intense scrutiny, we hear of so many apparitions of Mary from the accompanying visionaries who proclaim her message to the world. We need something extraordinary to convince ourselves that it is still safe to believe, that our lives are not self-deception, and that a loving God did create us and continues to care for us. We need something extraordinary to convince ourselves that God is still here. Whether or not such visions are authentic is not the point. The point is that they are popular because they appear to provide an anchor for the ship of our faith in the midst of a very stormy sea. And so we will flock to see weeping or bleeding statues, places visited by Mary, hear speakers to whom Mary has allegedly appeared. Although supporters would claim such activities are acts of faith, it is quite possible that they are more revealing of doubt than faith, a doubt that drives well-intentioned people to seek in extraordinary events the God who is with them always.

At the other end of the spectrum, there are those among us who withdraw into a world of quiet desperation

in the absence of extraordinary divine revelation. They may still engage in the ritual practices of faith but never cross the threshold from being churchgoers to people of faith. Since God has not eradicated the problems of drugs, war, hatred, poverty, abuse of power, and the like, they conclude that he probably does not exist, and that commitment would be a waste of their one chance at life. Maybe, like these people, we remain loosely connected to religion on the off chance that we are wrong or because we feel guilty, but such loose affiliation never approaches a real commitment in faith. When God does not fulfill our expectations, we turn away, preferring our own version of life. And so, in the absence of extraordinary divine intervention, we either seek God in the extraordinary with increasing vigor and devotion, or withdraw into a life of alleged faith that serves as a disguise, hiding our real suspicions and beliefs. Either way, we fail to open our hearts and lives to the God who is with us always. We fail to encounter him where he is most often found: in the ordinary of our lives and world. Once we discover God in the ordinary, we can begin to realize and appreciate the depth of his involvement in history and in our own history specifically.

The call of Moses

To discover God in the ordinary is one of the great lessons of the Bible. The call of Moses (Ex 3:4–22) is a compelling tale of one man's discovery of God's presence and will. The subtleties of the story of Moses' call are often overlooked, however. One such nuance involves the burning bush. Moses was tending the flock in a very arid region of the Middle East. In such a dry region, with the hot sun beating down, it is not uncommon for brush fires to ignite. That a bush would be burning in the region is not extraordinary. What Moses had undoubtedly seen many times before struck him differently this time. This time he saw the burning bush in a different way. This time the burning bush revealed to him the presence of the living God. It is not a talking bush but a religious experience, a perception of God's presence in the ordinary of the world around him that allows this story to speak to us now. In that experience in the desert Moses encountered the God of Abraham, Isaac, and Jacob, the God of his forefathers to whom the promise had been made and with whom the covenant had been entered.

In light of his experience of God in the ordinary event of a burning bush, Moses' first instinct was to reach out to his people, heirs to the covenant, who were suffering in Egypt. Living in the light of God's presence opens us to the needs of others around us. His presence calls us to reach out in love to others. Moses was no one particularly special, and by his own admission had no special gifts to offer his captive brothers and sisters. But, like so many throughout the Bible when they realize they are living in God's marvelous light, his openness to God's presence awakened him to the needs of others, and he was able to commit his life to the divine will. Regardless of what happened later in his life, Moses took his first steps to God by recognizing his presence in an experience of the ordinary. Appreciating this subtlety of the call of Moses can help the rest of us to recognize that each and every day we stand, as

Moses did, on holy ground. And, just as in Moses' story, we too can live differently in the light of God's presence.

The ordinariness of biblical symbols

Even the recurring symbols in the Bible speak more to the ordinary than to the extraordinary. Water, bread, wine, wind, light, fire, blood, and flowers are all rather ordinary substances or occurrences in human life. But, to the person open to God's presence, these ordinary, created substances take on a whole new life. They can be understood at a level deeper than the surface purpose that they serve. Water can cleanse us physically, but we are people in need of a deeper cleansing. Water can not only wash away our surface dirt, but the sin that mars our hearts and souls. Bread and wine can nourish and sustain us physically, but we are also in need of spiritual nourishment that can sustain our spiritual lives. Wind cannot be seen, but its effects can be felt; so too, the God in whom we believe is invisible, yet his effects can be genuinely felt. Light allows us to see where we are going and to recognize objects all around us. But we need to see our way spiritually and to see others the way God sees them. To do so requires a different kind of light, the light that emanates from the invisible God.

At the heart of these symbols is the biblical recognition that the world is so filled with the presence of its creator that even the most ordinary of objects can reveal the presence and love of God. The intensity of fire can speak to us of the love that burns in his heart for us. Blood can speak a word of freedom and life, just as flowers can communicate the beauty of God and the depth of his care for us. The biblical writers assumed that their audiences would understand the symbolic meaning with which they imbued a particular object. Although we are far removed from the world of the biblical writers and run the risk of over- or underemphasizing a particular symbol, we can learn a great deal from their choice of common, ordinary objects to symbolize the presence and love of God in the midst of a seemingly ambiguous world. The choice of such objects can inspire us to take a second look at the world and the people around us and see, as if for the first time, a people and a world filled with the Spirit of God.

This point was driven home to me in one of the most touching stories in which I have ever been involved as a professional minister in the church. It concerned a participant in the Christian initiation process. Not having had much involvement with faith and religion in her past, she had felt a void throughout much of her adult life. She tried to fill the void in a number of ways, and yet the void remained. Finally, with the help of a friend, she decided to explore the possibility of becoming a Roman Catholic. As it turned out, the initiation process helped her discover that the void represented her natural longing for God. At the end of the process, she was fully initiated sacramentally into the church community. Reflecting with her a few weeks later, I saw tears come to her eyes as she confessed why the process had touched her so. She said the process touched her because all of her life she had been looking for God in great signs, wonders, and miracles, and the process of Christian initiation helped her realize that, on occasion, the divine may be discovered there. But, most of the time we encounter God in each other, in the Spirit of God within ourselves. Not in miracles, not in the extraordinary, but in the ordinary encounters between people was where she discovered God's presence most powerfully. Like the apostles after the ascension, she had been busy staring up into heaven when God was with her all along.

Elijah at the mouth of the cave

Perhaps the most powerful biblical story of recognizing God in the ordinary involves the prophet Elijah (1 Kgs 19). Jezebel, queen of Israel in the mid-ninth century before Christ, sends a message to the prophet Elijah stating that she is going to have him killed. Jezebel worshiped the gods Asherah and Baal and had spread worship of these false gods throughout the land. Elijah, however, stands firm in his faith in God and, in a public contest, defeats the prophets of Baal, an outcome decidedly opposed to Jezebel's wishes. In anger, she threatens to kill Elijah for his work in damaging the cult of Baal and bringing glory to the name of God. In fear, Elijah flees the area and prays that God end his life. But, instead, he is led for forty days and forty nights through the desert to Horeb, the mountain of God. Once there, he finds lodging in a cave in which he again raises his cry to God. God tells Elijah to stand at the mouth of the cave, for he will be passing by. Elijah does so, and a great, strong wind passes by, breaking rocks into pieces in its wake, but God was not in the mighty wind. After the wind a powerful earthquake strikes, and yet God is not in the earthquake. After the earthquake there came a terrific fire, but God was not in the fire. After the fire Elijah heard a faint whispering sound and in that sound recognized the presence of God.

The enduring power of this story rests in Elijah's recognition of God in the faint whispering sound. Those of us who expect God to reveal himself in great, extraordinary signs could have waited for him at the entrance to that cave for all eternity and never recognized the divine presence. Why? God did not reveal himself in those things we might expect, and might want, to be the vehicles for such revelations. He did not appear in the remarkable. He did not appear in the way we may have expected. No, he chose to be revealed in a simple sound, a sound that revealed a presence many of us miss because our lives are so complicated and our expectations so lofty. It was not a miraculous sign or an act of great power, but a simple, ordinary sound that revealed to Elijah that he stood in the presence of God. How many times do we, in the course of a day, a week, a year, a lifetime, listen beyond the simple whispers in our lives in the hope of hearing God's voice bellowing in the wind, earthquake, and fire? In the midst of his anguish, Elijah did not demand a miracle from God, did not cry out to the heavens for a sign of power. Instead he sought him where he is most often to be found—in the simple and the ordinary. God's presence was so simple, so obvious, so ordinary that those of us in Elijah's place who would have looked for or demanded more could easily have missed it.

Peter's blindness

Elijah's ability to recognize God in the common and ordinary is underscored by a biblical example of the opposite behavior. When Jesus climbs the mountain and is transfigured before the eyes of Peter, James, and John (Mt 17:1–8; Mk 9:2–8; Lk 9:28–36), Peter wants to remain on the mountain and build tents for Jesus, Moses, and, ironically, Elijah, who have appeared to Jesus. Peter does not understand the significance of the vision. Earlier in the Gospels of Matthew (16:21–23) and Mark (8:31–33), after having listened to Jesus predict his own death in Jerusalem, Peter attempts to dissuade Jesus from going, an attempt that draws a sharp rebuke from Jesus. Peter understands neither the significance of the transfiguration nor what is to unfold in Jerusalem. Peter had an expectation of what and who the messiah should be, expectations that Jesus had begun to confound. Rather than allowing Jesus to inform his perception of who and what the messiah should be, Peter consistently tries to mold Jesus into his own image of the messiah and his own view of how God's eternal rule was to be fulfilled. Elijah was able to recognize God's presence because he was open to the ways in which the divine was present in the world, whether in the ordinary or the extraordinary. Peter missed the significance of the transfiguration and the prediction of Jesus' impending death in Jerusalem because he was too busy looking for the messiah in the manifestation he had expected and wanted.

God's presence in the ordinary

If we are honest with ourselves, cannot the same be said of us as well at times? Do we not create expectations of who God should be and how he should be revealed to us rather than simply opening ourselves to his presence wherever and however that presence is expressed? Do we not miss the divine presence in our lives because we hold to a clear set of parameters about his activity and presence? Unless it is extraordinary, God must not be here. Unless it is extraordinary, he must not exist or must not care. Like Peter, we take the chance of never knowing the presence of God in our lives because we have limited the ways in which we will accept his self-gift. As a result, we run the risk of never experiencing the tremendous joy of knowing God at a personal level and so are never able to commit our lives authentically to seeking and doing the divine will. Fortunately, Peter did not give up; he lived out his days confident of the presence of Jesus in the midst of his life, world, and work. Fortunately for us, we can learn a great lesson from the Bible. We can learn to open our hearts and lives to the Spirit of God dwelling within us and so learn to recognize God in the ordinary of life. We can learn from the call of Moses and from the ordinary symbols through which the biblical writers were able to share their experience of God's presence and love with others. We can learn from the example of Elijah, a prophet willing to open his heart and mind so totally to God that he was able to recognize the divine in the way God chose to reveal himself, even if such revelation occurred in a simple, ordinary way. We can learn from the Bible to look for God, not just in extraordinary experiences and events, but in the ordinary of everyday life: in the faith of others we encounter, in the tremendous good done by so many in the midst of a chaotic world, in the love we experience in our relationships, in the strength that helps us through the hard times, in the whispering sound of God within each of us. We just might find that he is more active than we previously believed. We just might find that he cares more than we previously thought possible. In opening our eyes and hearts to the presence of God in the ordinary, we just might discover the extraordinary love that God has for us all.

Exercises

1. Read 1 Kings 19:1–13a. Walk outside and spend a few minutes simply observing the wonders of the natural world. Open yourself up to the presence of God in the seemingly ordinary—the sky and clouds, the trees and flowers. If this is done at night, open yourself to God's presence in the moon and stars or the cool breeze.

2. Read Exodus 3:1–15. Try to cultivate an awareness of God's presence by recognizing that all of us are always standing on holy ground. Before starting each day and throughout each of your days, try to remind yourself that you are standing on holy ground.

3. Read Matthew 17:1–8. Reflect on the ways in which you and all of us miss God's presence in our lives and think about ways to increase our awareness of God's presence.

Chapter Two

God Present in the Midst of Evil

*P*erhaps the most enduring challenge to the life of faith and an openness to God's presence is the persistence of evil. Believers down through the centuries have struggled to reconcile their belief in a good and loving God with the experience of unnecessary suffering and evil. Evil is frequently cited as the reason why unbelievers reject God or the notion that God is good, loving, and present. Even for believers, the experience of evil causes many to pause and reflect on how it can remain such a powerful part of human life, given our belief in God's goodness and power. Our attempts through the years to answer the question of evil have, by and large, failed. And yet, we persist in our belief in God's presence and love in the midst of a world scarred by evil. We may not have any complete answer to the problem, but the wisdom of the Bible can strengthen us in our attempts to live as faithful witnesses to God's presence and love in spite of the reality of evil.

The experience of evil

Ann, by her own admission, had a wonderful life. She had a good husband and a beautiful daughter of whom she was enormously proud. She and her daughter, Beth, were best friends. They went shopping together, they went to dinner together, they enjoyed each other's company. Despite their closeness, Beth never lost sight of the fact that Ann was her mother, nor did Ann. She wanted her daughter to feel her warmth and care, and yet, at the same time, she needed to remain Beth's mother. Children have plenty of friends, she would say, but they only have one mother. For years Ann had been able to keep this delicate balance, and Beth grew into a mature, caring, young woman of whom many were fond.

All of that changed one early September evening when a driver, eager to enter traffic, did not pay close enough attention to what he was doing. He hit Beth and a friend as they walked home from a dessert establishment after having enjoyed an ice cream on that warm night. Beth never recovered from the injuries she sustained and died two weeks later. Ann and her husband Hank joined support groups to help them deal with their loss. They employed grief counselors to help them come to some level of resolution over their daughter's death. Entering their home, one could immediately feel the effects of the pall that hung over this poor, grieving couple. What they discovered through their support groups and grief counselors was that no amount of talking, no amount of sympathy could ever replace their daughter. They were simply going to have to learn how to cope with the fact that their daughter was gone and to find some way to feel joy in life again.

In the midst of their struggle to go on, Hank died. Ann, whose life such a short time ago had been so wonderful, now found herself waking up alone. She was all by herself. In the months and years following Beth's death she often found herself looking heavenward, asking God why. She examined her own life, hoping to discover the reason that God felt it necessary to allow such a thing to happen. She did not believe that God had caused the tragedies that befell her family but that God had allowed them, and she wanted to know why. When her question remained unanswered, she found herself remarkably angry with God. Shouting at him sometimes released the tension, but the question still remained unanswered, and it has remained so until this very day, over a decade later.

Where is Ann now and what is she doing with herself? She is a member of the Christian initiation team in her home parish, sharing her faith in God with those exploring the possibility of becoming Roman Catholic. Despite all that took place in her life, she remains a believing Roman Catholic, confident that God loves her and cares for her. She remains confident that God loves and cares for Beth and Hank, even though the answers she sought so vigorously have never been revealed. Some might say she is trying to deny the truth. But for Ann, the evil that befell her family is a mystery. In genuine faith, she knows in the midst of that mystery that God remains on her side.

Discovering a faithful response

The reality of evil remains the most common struggle for believers and the most common cause of distrust among those who doubt or do not believe. The popularity of such books as *When Bad Things Happen to Good People* testifies to the persistence of humanity's struggle with reconciling the reality of evil in our lives and in our world with our belief in an all-good, all-knowing, all-powerful God. Some see no need for reconciliation because evil is not real. Evil only appears to be evil because the finiteness of humans does not allow them to see that all things and events in the universe are really good. Others attempt to reconcile these seemingly contradictory beliefs by removing from God one or other of the characteristics traditionally attributed to God. They will argue that God can be all good or all powerful, but not both. Rather than explore the mystery for possible answers, they change the parameters of the playing field to avoid facing the daunting task of uncovering an answer faithful to the tradition in the Jewish and Christian faiths that God is goodness, power, and knowledge. Unfortunately, by changing the playing field, they offer a placebo to those who suffer. Such a placebo may fool people into believing that they have *the* answer but, over the long term, it does not remain faithful to the insight of the tradition.

The fact of the matter remains that, for the time being, there is no answer to the apparent contradiction of evil's existence alongside the presence of an all-good, powerful, and knowing God. To make such a confession would, for some, lead to a renunciation of their faith in God, or at least their faith in religions that profess belief in such a God. But, for many, to admit that we do not understand does not mean that God does not exist or does not care. For many, it means we must come to know God better, and perhaps by knowing God better, we might grow in our understanding regarding the reality of evil in our world. Certainly the biblical writers adopted such a view. Over the course of time the authors of the sacred books would come to recognize that they had no answer to the problem of evil. All of the answers offered throughout their history were soon seen to be inadequate at best and contrary to their beliefs about God at worst. And yet, the development of the response to evil throughout the Bible is one of the great lessons it has to offer us.

The probing faithfulness of Job

The most obvious example of the Bible's response to the issue of evil would be to speak of Jesus and his trust in the Father's love, even in the face of his impending death on the cross. There are other biblical examples of similar trust in God's providential care for creation. Job, although he does not live up to the stereotype most hold of him, fits the mold. In spite of all that happens to him, the Book of Job concludes by affirming his fidelity to God and his belief that trusting in God and God's plan is what is truly necessary in life. Job, despite the stereotype, does not sit by patiently as his family, his possessions, and his health are all taken from him. Rather, Job cries out to God, asking for justice, asking the same question—"why?"— that we ask when struck by tragedy. Job gets frustrated and depressed, angry and demanding. Like so many who have tried to live good lives only to have tragedy after tragedy heaped upon them, Job feels justified in his righteous indignation. He had done his best to be a good person all of his life, and his efforts succeeded since the Bible tells us that he is blameless and upright—an ancient Hebrew way of declaring that someone is perfect. And yet, despite his goodness, his world falls apart. He loses his wealth, his possessions, his home, his children, and he is afflicted with boils from head to toe.

For answers, he, like so many of us, looks to God— the God in whom he had always placed his trust in the good times. Friends come to comfort him in his affliction and pain, but with friends like these one does not need enemies. They eventually blame Job for his problems, claiming that his afflictions *had* to be his fault. He *must* have done something to draw God's disfavor. In our own time we hear the echo of Job's friends from the voices that declare the AIDS virus a punishment from God for the homosexual lifestyle. The author of the Book of Job would consider such a view hateful and opposed to the biblical view of God. The author of the Book of Job would be right.

Without the support of friends and surrounded by tragedies, Job turns to God to ask why. Angry at what has occurred in his life, he proclaims his innocence before God and challenges him for allowing such tragedy to befall someone like himself, who had lived a blameless and upright life. The fact that God does not really answer Job is not the point. The point is that Job never renounces his belief in God; he may be angry with God, but it is still God with whom he is angry. No matter the calamities that befall him, Job never relinquishes his belief in God, nor does his allegiance ever wane. In the midst of his calamities he does not stop believing in God, but in fact turns to God for help in understanding. The fact that such a turning to God was voiced in angry and frustrated ways misses an important message of the Book of Job. Job's fundamental choice in life remains unchanged by what has befallen him and his family; he will remain faithful to the God whom he believes loves and cares for him.

The Book concludes with God appearing to Job in a whirlwind and responding to Job's questioning, not with answers but with questions of his own. "Where were you when I founded the earth? Tell me, if you have understanding. Who determined its size; do you know? Who stretched out the measuring line for it?" (Jb 38:4–5). God chides Job for questioning the ways of the divinity; Job, moved by the presence of God, repents and renews his trust in the Lord. Such a conclusion might be disappointing to many of us who might appreciate more clarity from God. But, for the author of the Book of Job, the message is quite clear. If we believe in God we must trust God's promises, even when it appears they have no way of coming to be. Was not that one of the messages we could glean from the story of Abraham and Isaac? God promises Abraham descendants that will become a great nation. Isaac is the child of that promise, yet God commands Abraham to sacrifice his son. Abraham is willing to sacrifice Isaac because he trusts even when it appears that the promises of God have no way of being fulfilled. To trust in God completely is to accept that we will encounter situations and events that will not make sense to us. During such times we must not abandon our faith in God, but turn all the more profoundly to him. The Book of Job does not attempt to resolve the problem of evil, but it does provide us with a great gift, a way to live honestly and faithfully even in the midst of evil.

The suffering faithfulness of Paul

Job is not the only person in the Bible who suffers. Moreover, Job is not the only *just* person in the Bible who suffers. St. Paul suffers tremendously for his willingness to preach the Gospel. In his letters we are occasionally given some insight into the life Paul led and the suffering he endured as a result of his preaching the good news of what God had done in Jesus. On several occasions Paul was beaten almost to the point of death. He was imprisoned, stoned, mocked, abused, persecuted, and eventually beheaded. Of the many things people have claimed with regard to Paul, stupidity is not one of them. He was well aware of what awaited him if he persisted in his preaching of Christ crucified and risen. The attempts to stone him as well as the beatings he endured and the physical trials through which he labored were all indications of the life and death that awaited him. In addition, Paul suffered at other levels. Paul speaks of the thorn in his side and the covetousness that was killing him. Some have suggested

Paul was referring to physical ailments, while others suggest he was speaking of his wounded heart. Either way, Paul suffered for his willingness to preach the Gospel, for his willingness to follow Christ.

The experience on the road to Damascus that began the process of his conversion called him to a life of service and of preaching the gospel. Certainly, that life was to include much in the way of physical hardship and suffering for the sake of the Gospel. It also included mental and emotional hardship as he struggled to let go of his old life and his own wants and desires. He experienced all of this pain and anguish for preaching the Gospel, enduring all sorts of suffering and hardship. And yet, more than endure, he rejoiced in his pain and suffering because he saw in them his own sharing in the crucifixion of Jesus. For Paul, God's power is revealed in powerlessness, and his pain and suffering were expressions of God's power working through him.

We may not think like Paul did or even agree with Paul's outlook on suffering. To be grateful for pain and suffering may not strike us as representative of what God intended for us. And yet, there is something powerful to be learned from Paul's example. Like Job, he dedicated his life to God and strove to be blameless in God's sight. And reminiscent of Job, Paul's dedication to God results in suffering and tragedy. For his efforts he is beaten, imprisoned, stoned, mocked, and killed. In the midst of experiences of such pain and suffering, Paul did not question his allegiance to God but sought out God to discover the meaning of such suffering in his life. The trials he endured did not lead him to doubt God's existence or God's goodness. Rather, Paul lived through those moments, aware of God's presence within him and at his side. Paul did not feel abandoned or despairing in the face of evil. He knew that Christ lived within him as a result of his sharing in Christ's crucifixion (Gal 2:19–20). It was his openness to the Spirit of Christ within him that allowed Paul to recognize God's transforming power in the face of evil and suffering. Paul did not face his suffering without question, but his questions were directed to God. Like Job, Paul remained faithful to God even if he spent some time questioning the way his life was unfolding and the role of God in his misfortune and suffering.

For Paul, to be a Christian meant enduring pain and suffering at some level. He found consolation in the God who had become human and suffered a painful death on the cross. Rather than seeing God as an enemy and the cause of his suffering, Paul found in God one who suffered alongside of him and was an example for how best to live in the midst of suffering. Paul knew, as did the author of Job, that evil is a mystery. But, for those of us who must live with that mystery, Paul reminds us that God is on our side. God does not cause evil; God stands beside those who suffer. Paul appreciated at a very personal level the importance of the resurrection. The witness of the resurrection assured him that suffering did not have the last word, and that for those who remained faithful in spite of such evil, new life awaits. New life awaits them after death, to be sure, but also throughout life.

Examples in faith

Paul and Job can continue to stand out for us as shining examples of faithfulness in the face of evil and suffering. Neither of the two men came to believe without suffering, and neither remained in his belief without suffering. Recognizing God's Spirit living within them, both were able to recognize God's loving presence in the midst of evil and suffering. The power of the examples of Job and Paul lies in the recognition that they remained faithful to God, not because their lives were free from suffering, but because their suffering never diminished their hope in God and in God's goodness. Their hope that God would win out in the end, that he would speak the final word of their existence, allowed them to remain faithful even in the face of situations that severely tested their dedication and commitment to him. It was their faith in God's ability to redeem in this life and the next that strengthened them in their resolve to remain faithful to the God whom they believed loved them into existence. Their example can strengthen us as we strive to lead lives that reflect our hope in God's presence and love, not because our lives are devoid of suffering, but in spite of it. We can be encouraged to pursue more actively our mission to proclaim the Gospel, even in the face of suffering, strengthened in our hope by the example of those who have gone before us trusting in the ultimate goodness of God's love. Andy Dufresne, a character in the film *The Shawshank Redemption*, would concur, suggesting to his friend Ellis Redding that hope is the best thing and, like all good things, never dies.

Exercises

　　1. Read the passion narrative in Luke (22:1–23:56). Reflect on your experiences of the cross. Are you able to connect your experience of suffering to Christ's suffering on the cross? Can the way Jesus faced his passion and death help you to remain faithful to God in times of evil and suffering?

　　2. Read 2 Corinthians 4:7–18. Are you willing to suffer for the sake of the Gospel? Are you able to recognize the presence of Christ in your suffering? Reflect on the ways you can more profoundly conform your life to the life of Christ.

Chapter Three

God Works through Us All

*I*n the beginning of John's Gospel, when two disciples of John the Baptist approach Jesus inquiring about where he is staying, he invites them to "come and see" (Jn 1:35–39). The two disciples enter where Jesus is staying, come to know him better and then journey with him all the way to Calvary, Easter and beyond. But, for many, the erroneous thinking is that the offer made to those two disciples is not extended to us. The invitation to enter and stay with Jesus is an invitation believed to be extended only to those perceived as holy among us–priests and nuns and extraordinary laypersons, but not you and me. We think we are everyday people with every-day concerns. We are not called to holiness or discipleship; such things are for clergy and religious.

By accepting this line of thinking, faith becomes for many a matter of standing outside the door where Jesus resides, hoping to hear a word that might help us along our way. Such thinking leads to the conclusion that the call to enter is not for everyone; rather, it is extended only to those through whom it may be perceived that God works: the ordained, vowed, religious, or extraordinary layperson. As a result, discipleship for many is a type of vicarious living, hoping to reap the rewards of the holiness of others, those through whom it is perceived God makes his presence known. And yet, the Bible speaks a very different word. In the pages of the Bible we discover that the Spirit of God lives fully within each of us, the Spirit that calls each of us to holiness, that calls each of us to walk in the light of God's presence. In the message of the Bible we realize that staying with Jesus is not meant for clergy and religious alone, but is an invitation extended to us all.

One call

The Second Vatican Council echoed this biblical theme in the images it used to express the Church's identity and its mission in the modern world. Vatican II affirmed the biblical vision that we all share in the call to holiness. The Dogmatic Constitution on the Church uses the image of the people of God to express its understanding of who we are as a church.[3] It stressed that each of us receives the same call that those two early disciples received. Each of us is summoned to enter and stay with

Jesus. We are all asked by God to share our gifts for the good of the Church and the gradual transformation of society. When we only look outside of ourselves for holiness, we fail to recognize the Spirit of God living within us, calling us to embody his love in the world.

Vatican II took seriously the biblical vision that recognized us as a "chosen race, a royal priesthood, a holy nation, God's own people..." (1 Pt 2:9). St. Paul addresses each of us when he reminds his readers that we are all, at the most fundamental level, "one in Christ Jesus" (Gal 3:28). The biblical authors understood that God summons all of us to be faithful and to carry on the mission of Jesus his Son. Just as God loves us all, his gracious presence challenges us to respond, sharing with everyone we meet the love of God. As believers, we all share in the same call to spread the good news of what God has done for us in Christ.

That is not to say, however, that we all respond to God in the same way. Holiness is a call to which we can all respond regardless of our state or position in life. Through the centuries, the Church has been blessed by countless numbers of women and men who have graciously responded to the voice of God in their lives. Some have chosen to answer God's call through the commitment of married love or the single life. Others have chosen the path of religious life. Still others have responded as ordained priests or deacons. Holiness is not based on the roles we fulfill, but on the quality of our response to God's presence in the circumstances and situations in which we find ourselves. To be faithful disciples is to open our hearts to God's love and to allow our lives to be shaped by the power of that love.

Many of us still struggle to recognize and accept God's voice truly speaking to us. We perceive that our lives are not really a participation in the Church's mission to proclaim the Gospel of Jesus Christ. As a result, for many of us, our lives become compartmentalized; family life or career is distinct from our faith lives. While others are out doing God's will and sharing in the mission of Christ, we are making a living, paying the bills, loving and raising our families, and participating in other types of activities we perceive to be unrelated to the life and work of the Church. Many of us perceive our service to God's kingdom as limited to attendance at mass, providing for the religious instruction of our children, and perhaps attending the occasional parish meeting or social function. What is lacking in this view, among other things, is the myriad ways our lives can bring glory to God's name and peace on earth to his people.

Ordinary people, extraordinary mission

The third great lesson of the Bible is that God works through the lives of ordinary people. As I mentioned in the first chapter, it must always be recalled that we read the Bible through the eyes of hindsight. Moses was tending flocks in the field before he encountered God in the burning bush. David was a young shepherd boy at the time God called Samuel to anoint him king. The prophet Amos was also a shepherd before the Lord asked him to call Israel to repentance. We are familiar with the faith-filled lives led by so many in the Bible, but most of us know very little about the lives they led before God called them into service. Abraham was a wealthy family man before responding to God's call. We see him, however, in light of what he accomplished as opposed to the person he was. Prior to their conversion experiences, these biblical protagonists were ordinary people like you and me who happened to respond to God's call as it was addressed to them in the concrete circumstances of their lives. It is in the same manner that God's call is addressed to us all.

Abraham: Father in faith, father and husband

Being able to recapture something of the lives of many biblical characters before they responded to God's call is essential in helping us appreciate the reality that God's call is addressed to everyone. We see these towering figures of the Bible as great, as saints, only in hindsight, a privileged vantage point not open for the viewing of our own lives as they unfold. What God wished to accomplish through these saints of the Bible would no doubt have been a tremendous surprise to them, had they known of his plan beforehand. Both the Jewish and Christian faiths look to Abraham as their father in faith. Abraham is the great patriarch, the receiver of the promise of God. He was to be the father of a great nation, and the covenant into which God was freely entering with Abraham and his descendants would be everlasting.

And yet, what did Abraham do that God should have looked upon him with such favor? He moved his family and his wife Sarah gave birth to a son. He did not preach to the world in an attempt to convert them to faith in his God. He was faithful to the Lord in the midst of his life as a husband. Abraham was able to respond to God's call and to be faithful to him as a husband and father.

When it seemed as if he would not have children because of the age of his wife, the couple continued to express their love for one another, and from that love flowed new life, Isaac, the child of the promise. Abraham is our father in faith because he responded to God's call in the concrete circumstances of his life. There is nothing out of the ordinary about Abraham. He was not a man history would remember if it were not for his willingness to respond to God's call at a particular time in his life. The Bible reminds us that he was not a sinless man, and he certainly had his faults. But, the Bible does want to remind us that this ordinary man was open to God's call and responded to that call in the everyday occurrences of his life. That is what makes this ordinary man our father in faith.

Working through the unknowns of history

A more subtle approach to the lesson of God working through the lives of ordinary people is to be found in Matthew's Gospel.[4] The point is driven home in a section of Matthew's Gospel many of us may be inclined to skip over because it seems to have no spiritual value. In the first chapter of his Gospel, the author of Matthew provides us with Jesus' genealogy. He breaks Jesus' line into three sections, each containing fourteen generations. The first section is from Abraham to David, the second from David to the Babylonian exile, and the third from the Babylonian exile to the Messiah, Jesus. In the first two sections some of the great names of God's dealings with Israel appear, linking Jesus to Israel's great heritage. Abraham, Isaac, and Jacob, Judah, Ruth, Rahab, and Jesse are all significant names in Israel's history. Jesse is the father of

David and begins the second section of fourteen generations, a section including names like Solomon, Rehoboam, Hezekiah, and Josiah—all members of the kingly line of David. And yet, as we read the stories of those chosen to be included in the genealogy, we find that God has indeed written the story of salvation with crooked as well as straight lines. Jacob lied to obtain the birthright from his older brother Esau. Judah was among the brothers who sold Joseph into slavery. Isaac became the child of the promise while his half brother Ishmael was abused and mistreated. Despite appearing to fulfill God's promises during his reign, David, on occasion, resorted to murder to advance his personal interests. In reality, David's reign was the beginning of a process that ended with the Babylonian exile, a dim period in Israel's history.

I mention these well-known personages in Israel's history to highlight the identity of the final group of fourteen. Of all of the people in this final group, only two are recognizable: Mary and Joseph, a young girl and a carpenter. This final group consists of unknown people whose names never made it into sacred history for doing something significant. They are unknowns to us, people forgotten once they and those who knew them died. But, it was through these unknowns that God kept the promise alive despite the periodically mediocre response of those more famous in Israel's history. God kept the mission alive through those whom many would consider unimportant and utterly forgettable. God's message remained a living one through the efforts and lives of ordinary believers who quietly went about proclaiming the faith in the situations in which they found themselves. True, Israel's story needed its kings and prophets, but it was in equal need of ordinary people's dedication and commitment to God within the lives God created them to live.

The genealogy in Matthew's Gospel is an expression of hope as well as a challenge to all of us to accept our shared call to holiness and participation in the mission of the Church. The beginning of the story of our salvation involved the lives of saints and sinners, and sometimes the saint and sinner were one and the same person! If the beginning of the story involved saints and sinners, then the continuation of that story will also involve saints and sinners. The story will be continued in the lives of the Moseses, Davids, Peters, and Pauls through the centuries, but also in the lives of the Abiuds, Zadoks, and Eliakims as well. The odd assortment of people that contributed to the beginning of the story will also be present and involved as the story continues to unfold through the centuries. In that light, the genealogy is both consolation and challenge: *consolation* in that our lives contribute to God's mission in history, but *challenge* in that we must accept the responsibility to be heralds of God's good news in the world. In salvation history, no one is unimportant and no one is incapable of playing a role in making God's love known. The final section of Matthew's genealogy reminds all of us that the mission of God in history is carried forward by all who respond to God's love in the situations in which they find themselves. God's mission is entrusted to us all, and so we all share in the consolation and the challenge.

The backbone of a people

If we were to look at our own history as a nation, a number of names would easily come to mind. George Washington, Thomas Jefferson, Abraham Lincoln, Ulysses S. Grant, Franklin Roosevelt, John Kennedy, Martin Luther King, Jr., among others, are well known for their contributions to our nation's history. But, behind each great leader were those who did the grunt work, the ones who labored in the trenches day in and day out, in season and out of season. Their efforts helped to make the names we know so well so famous. Ulysses S. Grant is given a great deal of credit for waging the kind of campaign that led to the North's military victory in the Civil War. And yet, it was the effort and blood of thousands of young Americans working in the shadows created by the spotlight that brought about an ultimate victory. These were men who had wives and sweethearts, sons and daughters, brothers and sisters, mothers and fathers. Their names will never be recorded in the pages of history, but their dedication and commitment helped to forge an alliance of states into a united nation.

And so it is with the mission of Christ through the Church in our world. History will recall the names of popes and cardinals, saints and councils, but the mission of the Church continues to be advanced by the quiet efforts of those whose names will never fill the pages of a church history book. It is through the efforts of ordinary people, some of whom respond to God's call as priests and religious, while others respond as laypeople, married and single, that God's kingdom grows more recognizable. Jesus chose tax collectors, fishermen, zealots, and laborers to be the spokespeople for the good news of his love. Today, God continues to call laborers and lawyers, fishermen and firemen, tax collectors and trash collectors, and people from all walks of life to respond to God's call in the circumstances of their lives. The simple fact is that all Christians are called to be disciples of Christ no matter what their station in life.

Mary and the mission of the kingdom

Perhaps the greatest example of God's calling of an ordinary person to contribute to the mission of the kingdom is the call of Mary. Mary was a young Jewish girl without wealth or status. By historical standards she was one of the many ordinary people who walk the earth each day. And yet, God called this ordinary young girl to respond to God's love as a mother and a wife. It is within the environment of the family that Mary made her greatest contribution to the kingdom. By opening herself to God's call and responding to that call, she made family life holy. She made the ordinary tasks of family life an opportunity to spread the gospel message and to embody God's love. Through her dedication to her son and her commitment to God, Mary reminds us that the work of the kingdom belongs to us all. When Mary responded to God's call with the words, "Let it be with me according to your word," (Lk 1:38), she broadened our understanding of those to whom the mission is given. There is little doubt that the work of the kingdom and the call to be holy is a consolation and challenge that we all share. God's Word in Scripture seeks to encourage us to grow in faith and mission and to renew each day our openness to his call, that we might allow our lives to be transformed "according to your word."

Exercises

    1. Read Luke 1:26–38. How can you place your life in God's hands? Do you believe that God desires to work through you? If so, how are you willing to allow God to work through you?

    2. Read Genesis 22:1–12. What would you be willing to do for God?

Chapter Four

God Recognized
through Repentance

We are not who we should be. Both Jesus and John the Baptist knew this to be true. Both begin their teaching missions with the same announcement: "Repent, for the kingdom of heaven has come near" (Mt 3:2 and 4:17). Their call to repentance was not a matter of pointing fingers at the faults of others. For Jesus and John, the call to repentance was not a condemnation as much as it was an invitation. It recognized that we are not who we should be, but that we still could be. They saw the essential connection between accepting our sin and failure, and recognizing the love that God has for us. The fact that God is encountered through repentance is the fourth great lesson the Bible teaches. Through honest repentance, the human heart could open to the presence of God and life could begin anew. Such renewal is the basis of biblical hope. We have not been whom God has called us to be. But, through repentance, we can turn back to God, open our hearts to his presence, and be shaped by his faithful and abiding love.

A modern witch hunt

Self-esteem gurus hunt down negative thoughts the way witches were once hunted in Salem. Negative thoughts are a cancer that must be cut from the hearts and minds of humans if they are to experience health and wholeness. Years ago, I read a *Time* magazine article that challenged the thinking and advice of the popularizers of self-esteem philosophy. The article alleged that self-appointed self-esteem experts were subverting the health of our children by developing in them false notions of self-worth. Citing examples such as the midwestern school that gave each student the same academic award at the conclusion of each semester regardless of performance, the authors suggested that such strategies hindered the development of an authentic sense of self. The authors were quick to point out, and rightly so, that positive self-esteem is crucial to healthy living. What the article suggested was that popular strategies to develop a positive self-image resulted in the creation of a cocoon that insulated children from the realities of their own personalities and the world around them.

The article recognized a truth the authors of the

Bible were aware of over two thousand years ago. Recognition of the negative in all of us is necessary if we are to grow and develop as people. Denying that we are anything but perfect does not stimulate growth. Rather, it aborts it. The avoidance of any negative thoughts is really just fostering a lie about ourselves. There are many in the self-esteem business who appreciate the need to acknowledge that we are not who we should be. They rightly attempt to correct the problem in earlier thinking that did not respect the importance of a positive self-image and the need to nurture a genuine love of self. But, there are many, professional and nonprofessional alike, who believe that solving the problems of the world is merely a matter of telling one another how truly wonderful we really are. Children suffer from this kind of illusion. Such insulation from reality does not lead to positive self-esteem, but to a distorted sense of self. It is a sense of self that stagnates and avoids the maturation process by refusing to recognize the shortcomings we all possess. Such an approach to self-image does not cultivate genuine self-love and so ultimately leaves a person unable to reach out to others in love. We become people turned in on ourselves.

Create in me a clean heart

Unlike the popular self-esteem experts, the biblical psalmist knew the importance of accepting the fact that we are not who we should be. The psalmist knew there was a level of dignity to being human below which we should not fall. To deny that we fall was not only self-deception; it was sinful. It was sinful because it was aspiring to be less than who God had created us to be. It was forfeiting the glorious

God-given potential of human life. To deny our sin and failure was to remain in sin; it was to remain turned away from God. Admitting our guilt was not a condemnation but an opportunity for conversion. Only by accepting that we had turned away from him were we able to turn back to him. To live in the light of God's love required the development of an awareness of what it meant to live in darkness and of how that darkness expressed itself in daily living. Recognition of the effects of living in darkness renewed one's desire to live in the warmth of the light.

There is no better expression in the Hebrew Scriptures of this need to accept one's sins and failings in order to embrace the living God than Psalm 51. The New Revised Standard Version of the Bible states that this is a psalm written by David after the prophet Nathan confronted him regarding his adulterous act with Bathsheba. In this Psalm David expresses an honest sorrow over his act and admits his guilt in the presence of the Lord. And yet, his admission does not lead to wallowing in self-pity. Rather, David calls out to the Lord for forgiveness and a chance to start again. "Create in me a clean heart, O God, and put a new and right spirit within me." (Psalm 51:10) The recognition of his sin does not lead to condemnation or a further withdrawal into his own selfish desires. Instead, David's recognition opens his heart to the presence of God and to the possibility of new life.

Canceling the greater debt

The Gospel of Luke recounts an incident in the life of Jesus when he was approached by a sinful woman (7:36–50). While he was eating at the house of a Pharisee named Simon, the woman burst into the room and began to bathe Jesus' feet with her tears and dry them with her hair. Recognizing that the woman was a sinner, Simon doubted the authenticity of Jesus' message because he did not seem to mind being touched by a sinner. Jesus, knowing Simon's doubt, asked him who would be more grateful if two debts were canceled, the person who had been forgiven the greater or the lesser debt. Simon responded that the person with the greater debt would be more grateful. Jesus applied the lesson to the case of the woman and forgave her of her sin. What was important to Jesus was not that she was a sinner. What was crucial was that she recognized herself as a sinner and came to ask for forgiveness. It was her spirit of repentance that opened her heart to God's presence in Jesus, and, because of their encounter, she left with a peaceful heart and a new chance at life.

This story captures the substance of Christian hope. Christian hope is not wishful thinking based on fantasy and illusion. It is trusting that life can begin again, that the past does not condemn the present, that in the future all things are still possible. Christian hope is not concerned only with something we wish for after we die. It is trusting in God's love throughout our lives and allowing our sense of self to be shaped by that love rather than by our denials and self-deceptions. It is trusting in God's willingness to cancel any debt and embrace us in his mercy and love. As Christians, we speak of the Paschal Mystery, the mystery of Christ's dying and rising. The spirit of repentance that reveals the substance of Christian hope is the embodiment of our ability to share, not only in Christ's

death, but also in his resurrection. Jesus' resurrection does not promise us new life only after death. It is a promise of new life in the face of death's presence throughout our lives. A line of dialogue from Mel Gibson's movie *Braveheart* suggests to its audience that not everyone who dies has truly lived. The woman in Luke's Gospel was not truly alive, trapped as she was in a life of sin. Through repentance, she was able to experience the presence of God in the gift of new life. Her ability to rise from death to live in the light of God's presence offers hope to all of us that death may claim us at the end of life, but it will not claim us throughout life. In putting on the spirit of repentance, we encounter the presence of a loving God through whom we can rise to new life, through whom we can truly live.

Repent, for the kingdom of heaven has come near

The finest priest I have ever known, Joe, included in his homily at the wedding of my wife and me, a story about a family he had known and with whom he had worked. Joe was at the funeral home trying to offer some words of comfort and consolation to a woman whose husband had died, but he realized that the woman was not really paying attention. He asked her if something was wrong. She said that her daughter had just walked in and she did not know how the daughter was going to react to her father's death. "You see," she told Joe, "my husband and daughter had a fight seventeen years ago and they have not spoken since." (In case you are wondering why Joe told that story in the homily of our wedding, it was to emphasize the importance of forgiveness.) Neither was willing to seek forgiveness, and, as a result, seventeen years had passed between conversations. And now there could be no more talking. Not only did their unwillingness to seek forgiveness leave a wound that could never be healed due to the father's death, it had also tainted seventeen years of living. As we grow older, we become increasingly aware of the fragility of life and how quickly time passes. When we are young, life seems to stretch out in front of us seemingly without end. As we get older, we realize how quickly the future becomes the past, and how valuable each moment of life truly is. Imagine seventeen years of Christmases without enjoying time with your father or daughter, seventeen years of Easters and Thanksgivings with a very noticeable empty chair. Think of the many joyful moments a person can experience in seventeen years of life that would be tainted by the inability or unwillingness to share that joy with one's family. For both father and daughter, death had been a powerful presence, not only at the conclusion of those seventeen years, but throughout them as well.

The coming of God's kingdom is an opportunity for new life in God's presence. To accept Jesus' invitation to live in the light of God's presence requires that we recognize that we are not who we should be. Such acceptance allows us to open our hearts to God's mercy and forgiveness. Only by opening ourselves to the Spirit of God within us can we hear and accept God's invitation to start again; through the Spirit we can respond to the voice of God's Son calling to us to "come forth" from the tomb to new life. Through repentance we encounter the God who loves us so much that he never wants us to be lost. The father rejoices when the prodigal son who was lost is found. In repentance, the son recognizes his father again, and the father, in joy, rushes out to greet him. In the same way we encounter the presence of God, who comes out to greet us when we have recognized our sinfulness and have turned back to him. Such an encounter with God leads to an authentic new life in the Spirit of the risen Lord as opposed to the fake feel-good sentiments of the self-esteem gurus. The possibility for new life is the substance of Christian hope, a hope that death does not have the final word, that we can truly live in joy and freedom. Christian hope holds out the possibility that we can become who we were created to be. But, we can only become who we were created to be when we open our hearts and lives to the presence of God encountered in the gift of repentance.

Exercises

1. Read Luke 15:11–32. In what ways are you not who you could or should be? How do you experience new life?

2. Read Psalm 51. Are you willing to admit your sin and restructure your style of living to support your new life in God? What would be the substance of the new heart God will give you?

Chapter Five

God Present in Love

Thomas Merton once wrote, "Because God's love is in me, it can come to you from a different and special direction that would be closed if he did not live in me, and because his love is in you, it can come to me from a quarter from which it would not otherwise come. And because it is in both of us, God has greater glory. His love is expressed in two more ways in which it would not otherwise be expressed; that is, in two more joys that could not exist without him."[5] Merton understood clearly what the Bible teaches in numerous ways: God is present to us through love. To reach out in love to the other is not only an expression of God's love but it is a unique way of encountering his love. For Christians, the supreme expression of God's presence in love is the life, death, and resurrection of Jesus of Nazareth. Through Jesus are revealed the structure of human life and the spirit of human love. In our culture, when such emphasis is placed on the individual, the call to encounter and embody God's presence in love requires an urgent response. His presence is made known whenever genuine love is expressed. In such love God's presence becomes real.

Be all that you can be

Self-fulfillment. In our era, self-fulfillment has become one of the primary values in life. We are often encouraged to see what we do for a living, the objects we possess, and the relationships we develop through the lens of self-fulfillment. As a result, we will change jobs and careers more often; we seek ultimate satisfaction in what we own; we will move on to other relationships more quickly because our current bonds no longer satisfy us. Fulfillment can be sought through our career as an accountant or builder, as a secretary or nurse, by being the center of attention wherever we go, as a partner in a relationship or as an owner of some top-of-the-line product or a possessor of specialized knowledge. During my time of discernment in the seminary, students were often asked to reflect on whether or not life in the priesthood would fulfill us. Decisions can even be made by spouses and parents that reflect more self-concern than interest in the welfare of the marital relationship or the growth and development of the children. Self-fulfillment has become one of our most important values.

We live in a culture that encourages us to develop an exaggerated concern for our own welfare. Life is viewed through the lens of self-interest. Decisions are made based on how the outcome will affect me personally, even if I happen to be a spouse or parent. *Be all that you can be* is not only a motto for the army, but an expression of the spirit of our culture. Obviously, this is not the case for all people; those who are able to lead lives of genuine love do so to the extent that they are able to resist our culture's pressure to look out for number one.

I recall an episode from a daytime television talk show that concerned mothers who dressed rather provocatively. One mother was confronted by her ten-year-old daughter, who had been driven to tears on more than one occasion by the comments that her mother received because of her fashion choices. The mother met her daughter's tears with the suggestion that her daughter get over it. "It's my life and this is who I am. She's just gonna have to get over it," was the mother's response. It is an exaggerated example, but one that makes the point clearly. Many in our society are ruled by the passion for self-interest rather than guided and inspired by the spirit of genuine love.

To whom do our lives point?

Does seeking self-fulfillment make us bad people? No, but it does make us less than we could be and less than who the Gospel calls us to be. John the Baptist is an important person for the modern Christian to reflect upon. John is not only a person of significance in the Scriptures, but a prophet whose mission has been passed on to us through our baptism. As John preached in the desert and many came to be baptized by him, he knew that there was One among them whom they did not recognize. Just as John was called to help others experience the presence of the One among them whom they did not recognize, so too are we called to point to the presence of God in our midst by the way we live our lives. The Gospel of John relates an encounter between the priests and Levites from Jerusalem with the Baptist in the wilderness. The visitors from Jerusalem ask John who he is. He responds to their question by claiming he is not the messiah. John's response is interesting because he answers a question they did not ask. They did not ask him if he was the messiah, they asked him who he was. John's instinctive answer is to let them know up front that he is not the messiah. Why? John wanted to be very clear that his life was not about him and who he was. His life was about the One who would come after him. John's life is about the One to whom he points. They continue to question him, and he repeatedly responds, "I am not." In so doing, he underlines for them that it is not about himself but about the One who will be able to respond "I Am—I am the bread of life; I am the way, the truth, and the life; I am the resurrection and the life." The sole purpose of John's life is to help prepare us so that we may recognize the presence of the One among us whom we do not recognize, the One who answers our deepest and most profound questions by claiming, "I Am."

But it is easy to dismiss John. He was something of a religious fanatic who, although he was right about

Jesus, does not have much to say to us living today. He lived in the desert, so he obviously did not have to worry about a mortgage payment. People came out to the desert to see him, so he did not have to worry about buying a car and paying insurance. He did not have to worry about clients and customers and looking presentable, so he could walk around in camel's hair. On his own, with locusts and wild honey for a diet, he did not bear the responsibility of providing a decent life for his family. Jesus could be his primary concern because he had no other concerns, concerns that we have to deal with day in and day out. However, by focusing on that image of John, we miss the significance of his life and his relevance for us. If we focus on that image of John, we can keep him forever in the desert, dressed funny with an odd diet and no life of his own. In our attempt to dismiss John, we miss our call as Christians to be different, to be recognized not for our clothes and diet but for the degree to which we reflect the love of God in the world. Our primary purpose in life is to recognize that life is not about us. It's about our response to the call to reflect the One who is among us, whom we and others may not recognize. John, whose mission we directly share, reminds us that life is not about ourselves but about the presence of the One among us always.

To lay down one's life for one's friends

Since its inception, the cross has been the central symbol for the Christian faith. Jesus' death has stood at the center of our beliefs about God, humanity, good and evil, and ultimate meaning. In his death on the cross millions have found meaning and hope—hope that Jesus' victory over death speaks the final word about human existence. The cross can be a sign of consolation in particularly tragic times or even as we struggle to meet the daily responsibilities and expectations placed upon us by family and work. And yet, as in the case of the life of John the Baptist, even the symbol of the cross can be considered as irrelevant to human life. The way we speak of the cross can very often leave listeners with the belief that Jesus' death on Calvary was *pre-scripted* and that he had only to say his lines and everything would go as planned. Yes, death might be painful but it was part of the script, and Jesus knew the script ended with his resurrection. Death would seem to be nothing more than a long nap—the outcome of which—awakening—was never in doubt. To speak of the cross in this way can make it irrelevant to people who do not know the future and whose pain is all too real.

The cross is the central symbol of our faith, not because Jesus played the scene to perfection. It is our central symbol because it reveals the structure of what human life was intended to be. Rather than following the example of the self-interest of mythic figures like Adam and Eve, the love of Jesus embodied a willingness to live for the other, even to the point of sacrificing one's life. Created in God's image and likeness to live a life of love, we have chosen so often to seek our own fulfillment rather than that of our friend, neighbor, or enemy. In Jesus' death we see in an ultimate way who we were created to be. That is not to say that we should seek out pain for the sake of pain. What Jesus' death does say is that we must be willing to love, even when love asks us to pay a price. It is such love that reveals us for who we are, disciples of the God who walked among us.

It is very often true that our ends are in our beginnings. Jesus' end on the cross was foreshadowed by his infant beginning. The fact that his coming reveals the same structure as his death was understood and appreciated by the early Christians, who captured the spirit of both in a hymn that has been passed down to us through Paul's Letter to the Philippians. "Let the same mind be in you that was in Christ Jesus, who, though he was in the form of God, did not regard equality with God as something to be exploited, but emptied himself, taking the form of a slave, being born in human likeness" (2:5–7). The same concern for the salvation of all that led to the cross was evident in God's choice to definitively intervene in human history in the person of Jesus. The same structure of human life revealed by the cross was revealed in the incarnation, God's taking human flesh in Jesus of Nazareth. In the end, as in the beginning, Jesus revealed a God willing to pay any price so that those he loved might experience that love and reach out to others in the same manner.

Jesus and John

It was openness to such love that enabled John the Baptist to give his life so that others might know Jesus. Despite having developed a following of his own, he did not regard his own popularity and advancement as something to be exploited. Rather, he willingly gave his best, not for his own fame but to shed light on the One who was to come after him. Such selfless living brought many to repentance, but it also threatened to bring change. This threat to the established order could not be tolerated, and John paid the ultimate price for his faithfulness to God. His death was not a cruel end to a peaceful existence. It was an end foreshadowed by the life he had led, a life informed by the humble love of a God willing to risk it all so that we might live.

Jesus once said that John the Baptist was the greatest person to have ever lived. Yet, the least in the kingdom of God could be as great. Jesus did not die on the cross to reveal a love of which only God was capable. The cross is not an exception in human history. It is our defining moment because it points to the spirit by which we are called to live, the Spirit of God within us, opening our hearts to the Lord's love. It is the Spirit dwelling within us that allows us to live such love. The cross is not only the expression of God's love for us, but the structure that must give shape to our love if we are to fulfill the purpose of our lives. In the fulfillment of this purpose we discover the presence of the God who revealed to us in Jesus who we were created to be. Through lives shaped by the structure of God's love embodied in the birth and death of Jesus, we encounter the presence of the One among us whom we do not recognize. Through lives that do not regard self-fulfillment as something to be exploited, we both encounter and make known the presence of the God who became one of us to reveal his unfathomable love for us. The truth that we are capable of such lives is disclosed in the life of John the Baptist, who, as one of us, gave his life so that others might discover the presence of God.

Self-fulfillment and the presence of God

In the eyes of the Gospel, the desire for self-fulfillment makes us less than who we could be, who God calls us to be. It is not wrong to want a career that fulfills us and provides for our families, to look presentable and eat foods we enjoy, to seek relationships that will fulfill us and fill our lives with love. But the spirit of love revealed in Jesus' life and death reminds us that there is something in life that must guide our understanding and experience of these things. The structure of love disclosed by Jesus reminds us that all things—relationships, careers, and possessions—must serve, first and foremost, our call to encounter and embody the love of God in the world. John the Baptist reminds us that our lives are about more than ourselves. We may be fulfilled as an accountant or lawyer, teacher or student, priest or parent, but we are *Christian* lawyers and accountants, *Christian* teachers and students, *Christian* priests and parents. We may be blessed with loving relationships in our lives, but those relationships are gifts intended to reveal and reflect God's love for us all. Our lives are about pointing to the presence of the One among us whom we do not recognize. Our lives make the power of Christ's cross a reality whenever God is recognized—recognized by someone else because we have fulfilled our mission to be shaped by the structure of God's love for us. Life for Christians is not about self-fulfillment; it's not about ourselves. Life for us is about the presence of the God whom our love must reveal.

Exercises

1. Read John 1:19-28. How does your life point to the presence of God in our midst? How does your life not point to God's presence?

2. Read Philippians 2:1-11. How does your life embody or not embody the structure of God's love?

Epilogue

We are searching for the presence of God in our lives. For instance, consider the number and the frequency of the psychic hotline commercials that we see on television these days. It used to be that we would see their advertisements in the early morning hours. Now they appear on all stations at any time of the day or night. Psychic hotlines are growing in use and in popularity. Celebrities are used to endorse the hotline as if somehow starring on a soap opera makes them experts in supernatural affairs. According to some commentators, the horoscope is a more popular feature of the newspaper than the front page. It would be easy to categorize the people who make use of these services, but such a categorization might be unfair. We are seeking something tangible, something we can hold on to that lets us know that our lives have meaning. We want to know that there is something in the universe bigger than ourselves. We hear of believers from around the globe seeking out seemingly extraordinary phenomena to validate faith in a God who loves us. We want to know the presence of God in our lives, but we very often seek it in the miraculous and unique. If the miraculous does not occur, we can even create it on occasion. At root, we want God to shape our lives, even if we might look for his presence in the wrong places.

The Bible offers us a number of vehicles through which we can experience the presence of God in our lives. We cannot all be as lucky as Thomas, and have the risen Lord standing directly in front of us. The clear emphasis in the story of Thomas is the power of belief in the risen Jesus, sight unseen. With the eyes of faith focused in the direction that the Bible suggests, we might also encounter in a very real way the presence and love of God. God is as present to us as the risen Lord was present to Thomas. Rather than spending our effort and energy to prove God's presence, we need only open our eyes of faith to experience him in the world in which we live. By opening ourselves to the presence of God's Spirit living within us, we can encounter God in a very real way in the ordinary, in the midst of evil, through our shared call to carry on Christ's mission in the spirit of repentance and love. There are other ways to experience God that are expressed in the Bible and elsewhere. I have offered these five in the hope that they might awaken in you the desire to make the prayerful reading of Scripture a part of each day and to foster the openness to encounter God's love in your life and to share that love with others. After all, that is what being human is really all about.

Notes

All Bible quotes are taken from the New Revised Standard Version, New York: American Bible Society, 1989.

1. Source unknown.

2. William James, "The Will to Believe," in *The World Treasury of Modern Religious Thought*, ed. Jaroslav Pelikan (Toronto: Little, Brown, 1990), 100.

3. *Lumen Gentium:* Dogmatic Constitution on the Church, in *The Documents of Vatican II*, ed. Walter Abbott, S.J. (New York: America Press, 1966), chapters II, IV.

4. Raymond E. Brown, S.S., *A Coming Christ in Advent* (Collegeville, Minnesota: The Liturgical Press, 1988), 16–26.

5. Thomas Merton, *New Seeds of Contemplation* (New York: New Directions Books, 1961), 67.

ILLUMINATIONBOOKS

Other Books in the Series

Little Pieces of Light...Darkness and Personal Growth
> by Joyce Rupp

Lessons from the Monastery That Touch Your Life
> by M. Basil Pennington, O.C.S.O.

As You and the Abused Person Journey Together
> by Sharon E. Cheston

Spirituality, Stress & You
> by Thomas E. Rodgerson

Joy, The Dancing Spirit of Love Surrounding You
> by Beverly Elaine Eanes

Every Decision You Make Is a Spiritual One
> by Anthony J. De Conciliis with John F. Kinsella

Celebrating the Woman You Are
> by S. Suzanne Mayer, I.H.M.

Why Are You Worrying?
> by Joseph W. Ciarrocchi

Partners in the Divine Dance of Our Three Person'd God
> by Shaun McCarty, S.T.

Love God...Clean House...Help Others
by Duane F. Reinert, O.F.M. Cap.

Along Your Desert Journey
by Robert M. Hamma

Appreciating God's Creation Through Scripture
by Alice L. Laffey

Let Yourself Be Loved
by Phillip Bennett

Facing Discouragement
by Kathleen Fischer and Thomas Hart

Living Simply in an Anxious World
by Robert J. Wicks

A Rainy Afternoon with God
by Catherine B. Cawley

Time, A Collection of Fragile Moments
by Joan Monahan

15 Ways to Nourish Your Faith
by Susan Shannon Davies

Following in the Footsteps of Jesus
by Gerald D. Coleman, S.S. and David M. Pettingill